COOL
HELPING
CAREERS

SPORTS THERAPIST

By Geoffrey M. Horn

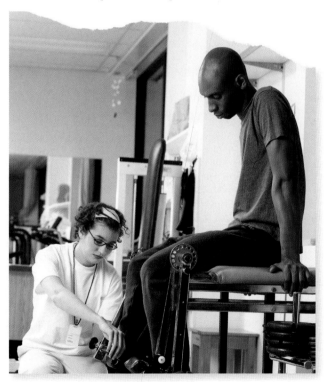

Reading Consultant: Susan Nations, M.Ed.,
author/literacy coach/consultant in literacy development

 **Gareth Stevens**
Publishing

Please visit our web site at **www.garethstevens.com.**
For a free catalog describing Gareth Stevens Publishing's list of high-quality books,
call 1-800-542-2595 (USA) or 1-800-387-3178 (Canada).
Gareth Stevens Publishing's fax: 1-877-542-2596

Library of Congress Cataloging-in-Publication Data
Horn, Geoffrey M.
    Sports therapist / Geoffrey M. Horn.
        p. cm. — (Cool careers: helping careers)
    Includes bibliographical references and index.
    ISBN-10: 0-8368-9196-1   ISBN-13: 978-0-8368-9196-6 (lib. bdg.)
    ISBN-10: 0-8368-9329-8   ISBN-13: 978-0-8368-9329-8 (softcover)
    1. Sports medicine—Juvenile literature.   2. Sports physical therapy—Juvenile
literature.   I. Title.
    RC1210.H67   2009
    617.1'027—dc22   2008014768

This edition first published in 2009 by
Gareth Stevens Publishing
A Weekly Reader® Company
1 Reader's Digest Rd.
Pleasantville, NY 10570-7000 USA

Copyright © 2009 by Gareth Stevens, Inc.

Senior Managing Editor: Lisa M. Herrington
Editor: Joann Jovinelly
Creative Director: Lisa Donovan
Designer: Paula Jo Smith
Photo Researchers: Charlene Pinckney, Kimberly Babbitt

Picture credits: Cover, title page: Hemera Technologies/Jupiter Images; pp. 4–5 Terje
Rakke/Getty Images; p. 6 © Steven E. Sutton/Duomo/Corbis; p. 8 Allen Einstein/NBAE
via Getty Images; p. 9 © Shaun Best/Reuters/Corbis; p. 11 Andersen Ross/Getty Images;
p. 12 © Pete Saloutos/zefa/Corbis; p. 13 The Meridian Star, Paula Merrit/AP; p. 15 UpperCut
Images/Getty Images; p. 16 © Steve Craft/Corbis; p. 17 Chris McGrath/Getty; p. 18 AJ
Mast/AP; p. 19 David Adame/AP; pp. 20–21 © Andersen Ross/Getty Images; p. 22 Drew
Hallowell/Getty Images; p. 23 (left) Gail Burton/AP; p. 23 (right) Jim Mone/AP; pp. 24–25
Juan Ocampo/NBAE via Getty Images; p. 27 Bryan Yablonsky/WireImage/Getty Images;
p. 28 Troy Maben/AP

Printed in the United States of America

1 2 3 4 5 6 7 8 9 10 09 08

CONTENTS

Words in the glossary appear in **bold** type the first time they are used in the text.

CHAPTER 1

SPORTS, FITNESS, AND FUN

Sports means different things to different people. For young players, it's a great way to get active and have fun. For developing athletes, it's a path to a school title or an Olympic medal. For top stars, it's a ticket to fame and fortune. For others, it's part of a smart plan to stay healthy and live longer.

All these groups have something in common. They want to get the most out of their bodies. Sports therapists help people achieve that goal.

Different Sports, Different Needs

More than 42 million Americans take part in sports. They run, bike, jog, skate, surf, swim, ski, and snowboard. Got a ball of any kind? People will bat it, bowl it, and throw it. They may also catch it, kick it, dribble it, or slam-dunk it. At a gym, YWCA, health club, or **dojo**, you'll find people doing aerobics, yoga, tai chi, or tae kwon do.

Whether the game is played for fame and fortune or just for fun, sports therapists help athletes get the most out of their bodies.

Eat right. Exercise right. Get fit. Stay fit. Millions of people of all ages, sizes, and ability levels are getting the message. Tens of thousands of coaches, trainers, and sports specialists of all kinds are helping to turn that message into action.

What Sports Therapists Do

"Therapy" comes from a Greek word that means healing. Therapists help people recover from injury or illness. They also teach people how to make their bodies stronger and healthier. People who improve their overall health and fitness are better equipped to avoid injuries.

Research shows about 20 million people are injured each year playing sports. Most of these injuries are minor. Some of them are preventable. Sport therapists can help players avoid injuries by showing them how to exercise effectively, warm up properly, and use the right safety equipment.

Injuries can slow anyone down — even a superstar athlete like Houston Rockets' Yao Ming.

Job Choices

Sports therapy includes many different kinds of jobs. Here are a few choices:

- **Strength and conditioning coach:** Helps athletes on school, college, and pro teams improve their athletic performance and **conditioning** through exercise.

- **Group exercise instructor:** Leads exercise programs for non-athletes in a group setting at gyms, resorts, hospitals, and employee fitness programs.

- **Personal trainer:** Works one-on-one with individuals. A personal trainer may provide advice on diet and nutrition as well as exercise. Job locations may include a fitness center or the person's home.

- **Massage therapist:** Helps ease sore or tight muscles. Work is done at sports medicine clinics, gyms, hospital and employee fitness centers, spas, and resorts.

- **Physical therapist:** Helps athletes with **rehabilitation** from specific injuries to muscles, joints, nerves, and bones. Work is usually done in hospitals, clinics, or private offices.

Sports as a Business

According to *SportsBusiness Journal*, sports is one of the fastest-growing industries in the United States. The U.S. sports industry is worth more than $200 billion a year. Spending to treat sports-related injuries totals more than $10 billion.

On the Job: Trainer/Coach Laura Ramus

Laura Ramus works for the Detroit Shock. She is the head athletic trainer and conditioning coach for this women's pro basketball team. She earned a college degree in physical therapy from Wayne State University in 1987. She then completed a program in sports medicine. Her team plays and practices at the Palace in Auburn Hills, Michigan.

What is a typical practice day like? "Generally, I have two or three people who need some form of treatment. All the ladies have their ankles taped. That takes up to 45 minutes. Practice starts around 11 or so, and it runs for two or two and a half hours. After the practice, I'll have two or three ladies who need to rehabilitate."

On game day, she's even busier. Players need to have their sore bodies taped and massaged. When does she rest? "When the game starts," she jokes.

Pro basketball trainer Laura Ramus of the Detroit Shock treats Cheryl Ford's injured knee.

At a U.S. Open tennis match, a leg problem gets immediate attention.

These job choices require different levels of training. Some demand a college degree, or even more advanced study. Others demand specific requirements that can vary by state, such as earning a **certificate** or license. Salary levels also vary widely.

Is Sports Therapy the Right Field for You?

Do you like sports? Are you interested in fitness, exercise, and health? Do you enjoy being around athletes? Would you prefer hands-on work at a gym, sports arena, or clinic to sitting in an office all day? If so, sports therapy may be the right career path for you.

CHAPTER 2

FITNESS WORKERS

Would you like to help people get fit and stay fit? A good way to do this is to become a fitness worker. In 2006, the United States had about 235,000 fitness workers. By 2016, that number is expected to increase to nearly 300,000. Fitness workers earn an average salary of about $25,000 a year. But a small number of top personal trainers can earn much more.

Getting Personal

Personal trainers work with people one-on-one. Some personal trainers have a large number of **clients**. They may see each client for only an hour or two a week. A few personal trainers work only with one or two well-known athletes or pop stars. In rare cases, if the client is very famous, the trainer may become famous, too.

When starting work with a new client, the trainer must find out some basic things. What is the client's age? Weight? General health? Overall fitness level? Is the client recovering from a specific illness or injury? How much time can the client commit to the program? Will the work be done at a gym or in the client's home?

Beyond these basics, the trainer needs to know the client's goals. Does the client want to improve his or

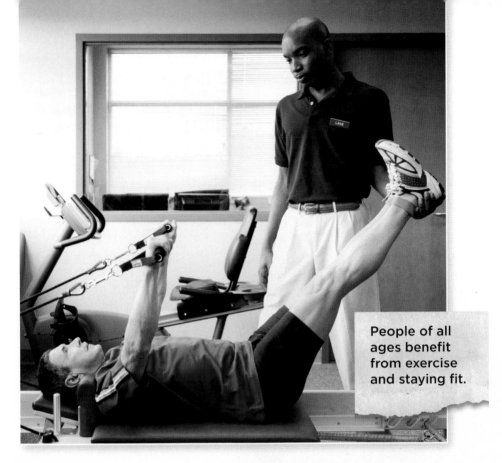

People of all ages benefit from exercise and staying fit.

her performance in a particular sport? Is his or her main goal to lose fat, gain muscle, or both? Which body areas does he or she want to improve?

When these goals are known, the trainer and client can agree on a plan. This plan may focus on improving strength and **endurance**. The personal trainer may offer advice on how to give up or reduce bad habits, such as smoking or eating too much junk food.

Working with Groups

Trainers in health clubs and fitness centers often work as group exercise instructors. Usually, group work is based on a particular activity. For example, some group workouts focus on **aerobic training**. These workouts are designed to strengthen the heart and lungs. They also improve blood flow throughout the whole body. Research shows that aerobic workouts can help people get stronger, live longer, and relieve stress.

Workouts may combine various bends, stretches, and dance moves. The instructor needs to make sure the exercises match the fitness levels of the group members.

Group workouts are an important part of many people's fitness routine.

How Trainers Get Trained

Where do trainers learn how to train others? Some trainers learn on the job. But many take programs offered by organizations like the American College of Sports Medicine and the American Council on Exercise.

You may need to meet some requirements before a training program will accept you. Typically, you must be at least eighteen years old. You must also know some basic first aid, including **CPR**. Some programs require a high school diploma. Others demand at least a college degree.

Programs typically provide a study guide or other materials. Then you must pass an exam. When you pass, you will receive a certificate. Some employers may ask you to get certified before they will hire you. Later, you may need to take more courses to keep your certificate up-to-date.

On the Job: Personal Trainer Bob Greene

Bob Greene is a personal trainer. He also writes books about health and fitness. He studied health and physical education at the University of Delaware. Then he earned a master's degree in **exercise physiology** at the University of Arizona. He belongs to the American College of Sports Medicine. He also is a member of the American Council on Exercise.

Greene became famous as a personal trainer for Oprah Winfrey. He helped Oprah lose 90 pounds. Later he helped her train to run a **marathon**. The job wasn't easy. "She's the first to say that she doesn't like exercise," he told a reporter.

CHAPTER 3

PREVENTING INJURIES

Injuries are no fun. They hurt. They slow people down. They break training routines. If not given time to heal, injuries may continue to cause trouble. Sports therapists help to prevent injuries from becoming long-term problems. They try to treat them quickly and effectively.

Getting a Doctor's Approval

Trainers and coaches can help prevent injuries in many ways. Before training starts, they may urge or require athletes to get a complete checkup from a medical doctor. First, the doctor will check the patient's overall health. The doctor will note the patient's age, weight, and how well his or her heart and lungs are working. Next the doctor will look for specific problems. These might include current or past problems with the patient's shoulders, knees, ankles, or spine.

Using this information, the doctor will then say whether the patient is healthy enough for sports or fitness training. The doctor may place limits on activity. Based on what the doctor says, the trainer may make changes in an athlete's exercise routine.

Exercising in a swimming pool can help patients recover from injuries.

Starting Slowly

Trainers need to make sure athletes warm up well. A good warmup is required before every practice, game, or training session. Stretching the muscles makes them more flexible. Muscles that are properly stretched are much less likely to become stressed or injured during a game or workout. They will also feel less sore when the workout is over.

Often, injuries happen when athletes try to do too much too fast. For example, people can get hurt if they try to lift heavy weights right away. The best approach is to start light and build up slowly. Good fitness trainers plan programs that last weeks, months, seasons — or a lifetime.

Avoiding Overuse

You can't keep working the same muscles hour after hour, day after day. If you do, you're likely to get hurt. A common injury among young pitchers is "Little League elbow." This happens when the elbow

A good warmup means lots of stretching.

Runners grab water from a drink station during the New York City Marathon.

Water Works!

When a person exercises or plays sports, the body loses water. Most of this water is lost through sweat. Athletes who lose too much water suffer from **dehydration**. Dehydration puts great strain on the body. It can make a person play poorly. And it can make someone very sick. Trainers and coaches must make sure athletes get enough to drink. They need to provide water or sports drinks before, during, and after exercise.

gets sore from too much throwing. A sore shoulder (sometimes called "swimmer's shoulder") is another injury that comes from overuse.

Sports therapists have ways to prevent such injuries. Good coaches take a balanced approach to training.

Excellent training helps
U.S. Olympic winner
Michael Phelps guard against
"swimmer's shoulder" and
other overuse injuries.

They vary the exercises so particular joints and muscle groups aren't overstressed. Sometimes these stresses come from flaws in an athlete's technique. Coaches can prevent injuries by understanding and correcting those flaws.

Another source of overuse injuries is incorrect equipment. For example, runners who don't wear good running shoes can develop leg and foot problems. Good trainers make sure athletes are using the right shoes and other equipment.

Playing Safe

Many sports require special equipment. Football players wear helmets and heavy padding. Skaters wear helmets, elbow pads, kneepads, and wrist guards. Soccer players wear shin guards and special shoes.

A trainer can help prevent injuries by making sure athletes are using the right equipment.

In the fitness center, a trainer can prevent injuries by showing people how to use equipment the right way. Treadmills and weight machines can be dangerous if people don't follow sensible rules.

Free weights can also pose a hazard. Someone lifting a heavy barbell must have one or two "spotters" nearby. These spotters need to act immediately if the lifter loses control of the barbell. This prevents the barbell from smashing into the lifter's face or chest.

Running back Javarris James of the University of Miami gets fitted for a new set of shoulder pads.

CHAPTER 4

HANDS ON

Many sports therapists do hands-on work with athletes. They tape athletes' sore knees. They massage athletes' tired muscles. They use physical therapy to help athletes recover from injuries. They provide first aid when an injury occurs.

Massage Therapy

Massage has been used as a therapy for thousands of years. It relieves stress. It makes sore muscles feel better. It can even help heal some injuries.

Athletes get massages to help them relax before a game. They also get massages after a game to relieve muscle stiffness. There are more than eighty different types of massage. Some methods require very strong hands. Others are more gentle and soothing.

Nearly 120,000 people have full-time work as massage therapists. Another 80,000 do part-time work. Some have jobs in spas, salons, health centers, and hotels. Many are self-employed. Most states require massage therapists to get a license. They earn the license by taking courses and passing an exam.

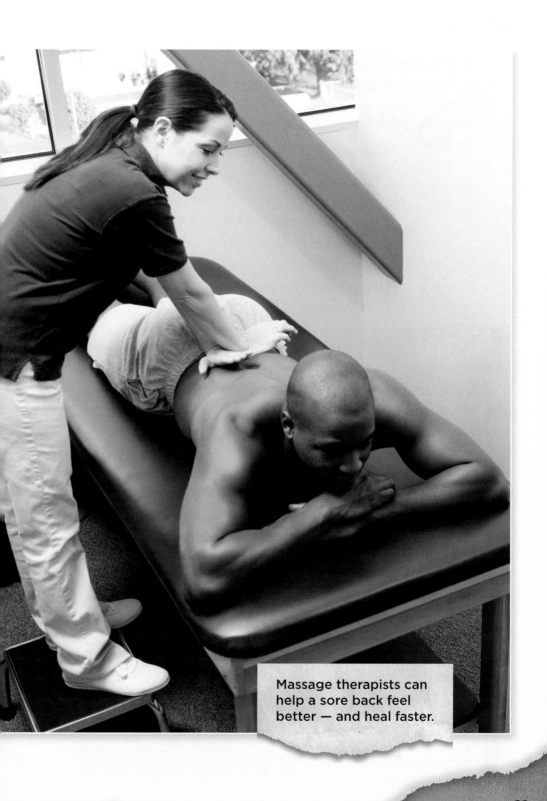

Massage therapists can
help a sore back feel
better — and heal faster.

On the Job: Massage Therapist Kathy Sherrill

Kathy Sherrill has worked as a massage therapist with the Philadelphia Eagles. She helped to heal the battered bodies of top football stars such as Terrell Owens and Donovan McNabb. "The guys are so knotted up after a game," she explains. "You've gotta push deep into the muscle to release it again."

The hard hits he takes on the football field have made Philadelphia Eagles' quarterback Donovan McNabb a big fan of massage therapy.

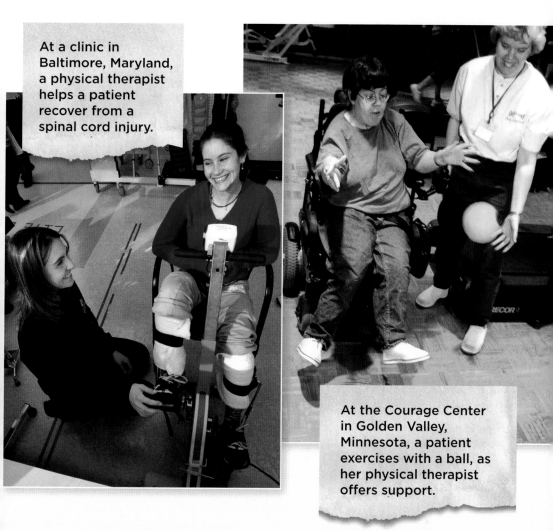

At a clinic in Baltimore, Maryland, a physical therapist helps a patient recover from a spinal cord injury.

At the Courage Center in Golden Valley, Minnesota, a patient exercises with a ball, as her physical therapist offers support.

Physical Therapy

Injured athletes need physical therapy. So do many other people stricken by injury or disease. For example, physical therapy may help someone with a serious leg problem learn to walk again. Physical therapists often help people improve their balance after an injury or an operation. Physical therapists also help healthy people who have special needs get more out of life.

Physical therapists have many tools to reduce pain and promote healing. Massage is one of those tools. Exercise is another. For an injured patient, exercise may be painful and difficult. A therapist's encouraging words help patients work harder — and recover faster.

Some therapists specialize in sports medicine. Others may choose to work with the very young or the very old. All physical therapists must have an advanced degree. They also need a license from the state where they work. To earn this license, they must pass an exam.

Getting Right with RICE

Scrapes, cuts, bumps, and bruises happen in every sport. Trainers, coaches, and therapists need to know basic first aid. Sports therapists are trained to know if an injury is serious, or if an athlete can continue to play. They recognize when an injury needs a doctor's care. But many mild injuries may be treated with RICE. The four letters in RICE stand for rest, ice, **compression**, and **elevation**. Here is how RICE works:

- **Rest:** Have the athlete take weight and stress off the injured part.

- **Ice:** Have the athlete apply a cold pack or ice bag to the injured area. Ice can be applied fifteen minutes at a time, four to six times a day. This will help reduce swelling.

Taping players' ankles is the basketball trainer's responsibility.

- **Compression:** Wrap the injured area with an elastic bandage. This also will help keep swelling down.

- **Elevation:** Have the athlete raise the injured body part above the level of the heart. This reduces internal bleeding around the injury.

Most minor injuries heal quickly when the RICE method is properly used. Serious injuries also require a trip to a doctor's office, medical clinic, or hospital.

CHAPTER 5

ON THE CUTTING EDGE

Would you like to become a doctor? Do you love sports? It's possible to combine both interests with a career in sports medicine or research.

This career choice is not easy. Many years of study are required. You'll need an advanced degree. But you'll have the thrill of helping athletes train better and play better than ever before.

Tommy John Surgery

In 1974, Tommy John was a left-handed pitcher playing for the Los Angeles Dodgers. John had a terrible problem. He had torn a **ligament** in his left elbow. With an injury like that, most pitchers had to retire. But John wasn't ready to quit. That year, he went to see Dr. Frank Jobe. He asked Dr. Jobe to find a way to repair the elbow.

Dr. Jobe did something radical. He took a healthy **tendon** from John's forearm. Then he drilled small holes in John's elbow. The tendon was looped through the small holes and attached to the elbow. That way, the tendon could replace the damaged ligament.

New York Yankees' relief pitcher Mariano Rivera had Tommy John surgery while he was still in the minor league.

John needed many months of rehab. But he went on to have a great career. Many top pitchers in the game today have had Tommy John surgery.

New Techniques

Knees take a pounding in many sports. Knee problems have cut short the careers of many football and basketball stars. For running backs, a torn knee ligament is a big threat. Fortunately, doctors have found a way to deal with this injury. They use a method similar to Tommy John surgery — only on the knee rather than the elbow.

On the Job: Sports Surgeon Lewis Yocum

Dr. Lewis Yocum has many years of medical training. He works at the Kerlan-Jobe Clinic in Los Angeles, California. He also serves as team doctor for the Angels baseball club in Anaheim.

Dr. Yocum has done many Tommy John surgeries. Most of the operations have been successful. "Guys go into the operation hoping for a cure," he says. "We're able to help the vast majority of them."

Arthroscopic surgery is another huge medical advance. This method uses a tiny tool that can look deep inside the body. The same tool can also help repair many knee problems. The surgeon can do the whole job with only a few small cuts, or **incisions**. Because the cuts are small, the healing is very rapid.

Today, doctors are inventing new tools and techniques. These high-tech methods will help more athletes play better and longer.

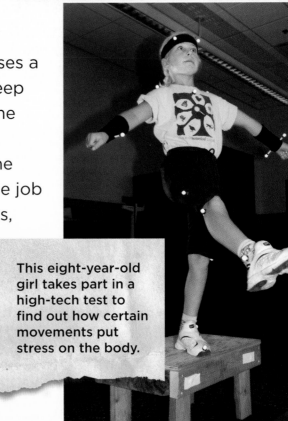

This eight-year-old girl takes part in a high-tech test to find out how certain movements put stress on the body.

SPORTS THERAPIST

OUTLOOK

- Sports is one of the fastest-growing businesses in the United States. People spend more than $10 billion a year to treat sports-related injuries.
- Jobs in sports therapy include personal trainer or group exercise instructor, athletic trainer or coach, massage therapist, and physical therapist. Some doctors specialize in sports medicine. Demand for all these jobs is increasing.

WHAT YOU'LL DO

- For some jobs — for example, strength coach or group exercise director — you may work with groups of people.
- For other jobs — personal trainer, massage therapist, or physical therapist — you'll do hands-on work with individuals.
- Specialists in sports medicine use advanced techniques for research and treatment.
- Work settings may include fitness centers, gyms, hospitals, clinics, or private homes.

WHAT YOU'LL NEED

- Therapists of various types may need to have a college degree or complete a special training program.
- Careers in sports medicine require advanced degrees.
- Fitness coaches should be physically fit. You'll want to set a good example.

WHAT YOU'LL EARN

- Salaries vary greatly. An entry-level position pays between $25,000 and $35,000 a year. Specialists in sports medicine earn much more. A very few diet and fitness experts have become millionaires.

Sources: U.S. Department of Labor, Bureau of Labor Statistics; *SportsBusiness Journal*

GLOSSARY

aerobic training — exercises designed to improve the heart, lungs, and blood flow

arthroscopic surgery — a method that uses a tiny instrument to allow a surgeon to look inside a joint and operate on it

certificate — a document stating that you have met certain minimum requirements for a particular job

clients — people who use professional services, such as those offered by a sports therapist

compression — in treating an injury, the use of an elastic bandage to keep swelling down

conditioning — physical exercises designed to improve strength and endurance and to prevent injuries

CPR — short for cardiopulmonary resuscitation; in a medical emergency, a method for restoring someone's normal breathing and heartbeat

dehydration — severe water loss

dojo — a school for martial arts training

elevation — reducing blood flow to an injured body part by raising the part above heart level

endurance — the ability to do something for a long time

exercise physiology — the scientific study of how physical activity affects the human body

incisions — cuts made by a surgeon

ligament — the tough material inside the body that connects bones to each other and holds a joint together

marathon — a race of about 26 miles (42 kilometers)

rehabilitation — a program designed to aid recovery from injury, illness, or abuse; often shortened to "rehab"

tendon — the strong material inside the body that connects a muscle to a bone